contemporary floral art

Ryusaku Matsuda

contemporary floral art
Ryusaku Matsuda

stichting
kunstboek

Introduction

Most of the works collected in this book are created by Ryusaku Matsuda, as a contemporary artist, for the purpose of this publication.

When I publish a book, I need the input from my old work to make my concept more understandable. The works published in this book are not ordered in a chronological way, but sometimes you can feel or see stories through them.

In my heart I am a contemporary Ikebana artist. I first learned the techniques and skills of floristry or floral art and – needless to say – of Ikebana, the traditional Japanese floral culture.

During my teenage years, I was intent on oil painting and thought about entering an art course at university. But I did not want to study the fine arts in an academic way so in the end I decided not to go to university. Although I am still not sure why I made that decision, I am sure that I made the right one. Because of it, I am open to any kind of beauty. And more than anything, it is my great pleasure to use plants as materials to express my art.

Several paintings that I made during my teenage years still exist. But the art works that I made in my thirties, using plant materials, are gone or have changed with time. I cannot help thinking that those works are more beautiful now than at the time they were created. Some people point out that those works got dirty or were damaged, but I hope that they will return to the soil at the end of their life, as I will return there too. I believe that my works change continuously as time goes by, and become more beautiful. I am not seeking eternity for my works nor fleetingness in an installation of a kind of contemporary art. I simply have chosen plant materials for my art representation.

Expressing plants as just 'plants' is not enough to call my work contemporary art. My essential concept, 'the passage of time', never changes, but what I show or create as an artist, must represent the times of today. Creating works responding to the present times, is a demanding reality, but if you have made a choice, you must be able to endure the implications.

After I have finished a work, I always mull over the fact whether it reflects the times it was made in, or not. I have never thought that I succeeded. There remains only the determination to try harder with the next work.

I want to explain why I would rather be called a contemporary Ikebana artist. As I stated above, I renounce the academic art education. I have gained my sense of beauty through plants. I have cultivated this sense by the symbiosis of the plants' life and mine. This is common to Ikebana's mentality and philosophy.

In Japan, we do not say 'to arrange or decorate plant materials'. We use the word *Ikeru*. That word cannot be translated into one English word.

Explained simply, *Ikeru* means making use of plants and at the same time making yourself alive, or showing expressions of your way of life. Therefore, in contemporary art, for me the verb 'to create' equals Ikeru.

However, a paradox is inherent to *Ikeru*. Both floral arrangements and Ikebana use plants as materials. These plants, when taken from nature, are killed. Next, the arrangement or *Ikeru* brings those same materials back to life. So we kill plants, to revive them later. We watch the process of decay and death of plants.

Of course, Ikeru is a source of pleasure to me, but I have started doubting to give myself over to that pleasure. That hesitation made me create the works in this book.

My works have possibly been getting away from (traditional) Ikebana and may show my unique view on life and death. The works are beautiful in colour, shape, material and composition. Constructing my own world beyond those matters is my purpose and meaning in life.

Most of my works are created by combining and piling up tiny pieces of material (thorns, petals, etc). Collecting, preparing and composing my works is a very time consuming process. It usually takes me three months to one year to prepare for an exhibition. I hold one solo exposition every year, but most of the time I am in the process of creating. When people ask me why I take so much time for my work, I let them know that touching plants, getting to know and understand them or just being around plants is my greatest pleasure. Plants have become my life. This is my way of living and I do not regret it.

Lastly, I am very thankful for being born in Japan. Our country is warm and humid and has a sumptuous vegetation. Ikebana came into existence by treating plants religiously, contrary to the farms that grew plants for practical use and support. Because of my being Japanese I am able to use a lot of flowers, trees and branches without destroying nature. All plants used in this book are purchased from the flower market. With this book the Japanese floral culture will not be global physically, but it will be mentally.

I sincerely hope you will enjoy my work.
Ryusaku Matsuda

Profile – Ryusaku Matsuda

1948	Born in Takasago City Hyogo pref. Japan
1970	Qualified as an instructor of Mami Flower Design School
1976 - 77	Studied in Europe ('82)
present	Head of Studio Matsuda 93
	Instructor at National University of Chiba in Horticulture
	Instructor at JFTD Japan Flower College
	Judge for Japan Cup (from 1991 until now)

EXHIBITIONS

1980	Contemporary IKEBANA Art Exhibition 1980, Matsuya Ginza, Tokyo
1981	"IKEBANA EXPO TOYOTA", Toyota Community Hall, Aichi
1984	Solo Exhibition, Ai Gallery, Tokyo ('85)
1986	Solo Exhibition, G Art Gallery, Tokyo ('87, '90)
1988	Solo Exhibition, Gallery Q, Tokyo
	Japan Display Design Contest Prize for Window Division
1989	"Contemporary IKEBANA '89", Matsuya Ginza, Tokyo
1990	"Flower EXPO '90" Art Director for Japanese Government's Garden, Osaka
1994	Solo Exhibition, Maki Tamura Gallery, Tokyo
	"IKEBANA as Expression" Nagoya Municipal Gallery, Aichi pref.
	Solo Exhibition, Art Forum Yanaka, Tokyo ('95, '97, '99, 2001)
1995	Solo Exhibition, Mobach, the Netherlands
	"Today's Japan" Sculptor's Center, Toronto, Canada
1996	Permanent Collection, Floral Art Museum, Chiba
1999	Art Director for Yamazaki kota Contemporary Dance Performance
2001	Solo Exhibition, "Curated by Mizutani Takashi", Gallery Maki, Tokyo
2003	"Perfection/Impermanence Contemporary IKEBANA", Glyndor Gallery, Wave Hill, New York
2005	"Zenkoji Great Flower Exhibition", Zenkoji Temple, (UNESCO world heritage site), Nagano
	Solo Exhibition "Spirit of trees", Tokyo Forum EXHIBITION SPACE, Tokyo
2006	Solo Exhibition "Bamboo World-Form of Air", Sasabunosato, Abekamaboko, Miyagi
	"Echigo-Tsumari Art Triennial", Niigata
2008	Solo Exhibition "My lovely Bamboo", Tokyo Forum EXHIBITION SPACE, Tokyo

PUBLICATIONS

1989	"Contemporary IKEBANA", Hachette Fujingaho
	"Flower Interior", Gakken
1993	"Hana Awase Iro Awase" Vol.1, Vol.2 Rikuyosha
1995	"Matsuda Ryusaku", Kyoto Shoin
1999	"World Flower Artist", Sodo Publication
2004	"Arrange the Seasonal Flowers", Kodansha

Bamboo

In Japan, bamboo is part of our lives. It is a plant with a high cultural significance and just like pine, it is considered the bearer of good fortune, prosperity and luck, especially at the beginning of the new year. Bamboo clearly shows its verticality and splits easily, therefore a person who is very straightforward is said to be 'like a split bamboo'. Bamboo has always been used in Ikebana and traditional Japanese flower arrangements or Ikeru.

While other forests are disappearing at a frightening rate, bamboo forests are spreading, both in number and in size. Bamboo is an incredibly quick grower, creating impenetrable green walls when left alone. For this reason, it is relatively easy for me to get permission to cut down bamboo in the forest. There are many bamboo forests around Tokyo, but finding the thick stems I need for my art, is not easy.

These are recent works. My Ikeru has evolved and improved over time, so I decided it deserved its place in this book. However, that does not mean that I am satisfied with it. Page 9 carries a special memory for me. When I received the bamboo it was so beautiful that I decided to put it in a vase and to take no further action. The only thing I did was helping the bamboo to stand upright.

I could see the original shape of the bamboo, with its strong roots in the earth, growing straight into the sky, leaves and branches trembling in the breeze. Breaking the joints and putting it in water made it possible to keep the bamboo in its original shape for three months. With this bamboo I could have performed Ikeru for the first time, but I didn't. However, by introducing me to the wonderful world of transformed bamboos, this work was pivotal for the rest of my career as a contemporary Ikebana artist.

stretch up – [p9]
Phyllostachys heterocycla 'Bicolor' | 1500 mm | 2008

to IKERU bamboo [p10]
Lilium longiflorum 'Takasago', Phyllostachys heterocycla 'Bicolor' | 2500mm | 2006 solo exhibition, Sasabunosato Abekamaboko, Miyagi

to IKERU bamboo II [p11]
Lilium longiflorum 'Takasago', Phyllostachys heterocycla 'Pubescens' | 2000mm | 2006 solo exhibition, Sasabunosato Abekamaboko, Miyagi

Bamboo

I have always tried to use bamboo in a different way than my Ikebana predecessors. Before I was forty, I had already given more than ten bamboo expositions. But after a while, I got the feeling that I had exhausted all possibilities of the material.

All I ever seemed to be doing was to cut, chop and chisel; to enlarge bamboo or to reduce it. In the end I completely stopped using it. I was sure I had grasped the sheer essence of bamboo.

Twenty years later, while working on this book, I got the request to make another bamboo piece to celebrate the start of a new year. It took me three months to finish the piece, but more importantly, it triggered off a fresh interest in bamboo.

In twenty years, I changed a lot, both mentally and physically, so when I tried to create the same works as before, I could not get the feeling right. I lacked the strength and sharpness. The resulting work was more gentle, as if I was healed by my own works. Contrary to my early works, I let the material itself decide what shape it wanted to be.

When I heard that the assistant who had collaborated with me 21 years ago, had kept one of my early bamboo works, I was thrilled. (The work is the smallest one on pages 22-23.) After twenty-one years it had experienced quite a transformation: it had changed colour completely and the surface was slightly cracked. It was time that had created this piece. The old work looked sharp and very powerful compared to my recent bamboo creations.

To show people the big changes time can bring about, I confronted both pieces in an exposition.

Even when I only need the trunk of a bamboo, the plant is delivered at my place with the branches and leaves included.

If I use a saw, there is dust. If I use a chisel, there are fine slithers of wood. Every single piece of material, even wood dust, is valuable. Nothing is wasted, I collect and keep everything. I have made works from all possible parts of the plant, but what I like most about bamboo is its tension.

I feel and see the shape of the air that is enclosed in or captured by the bamboo stems. With this work I wanted to see how the shape of the air changes as time goes by. When tension is lost, the air loses its clear shape, becomes unpredictable and - in the end - is returned to the earth.

These specific works didn't change too much after one month. The photo was taken when it had just been created, so it is still a powerful shape of air. It was too big to keep and I regret not having photographed it after the exhibition.

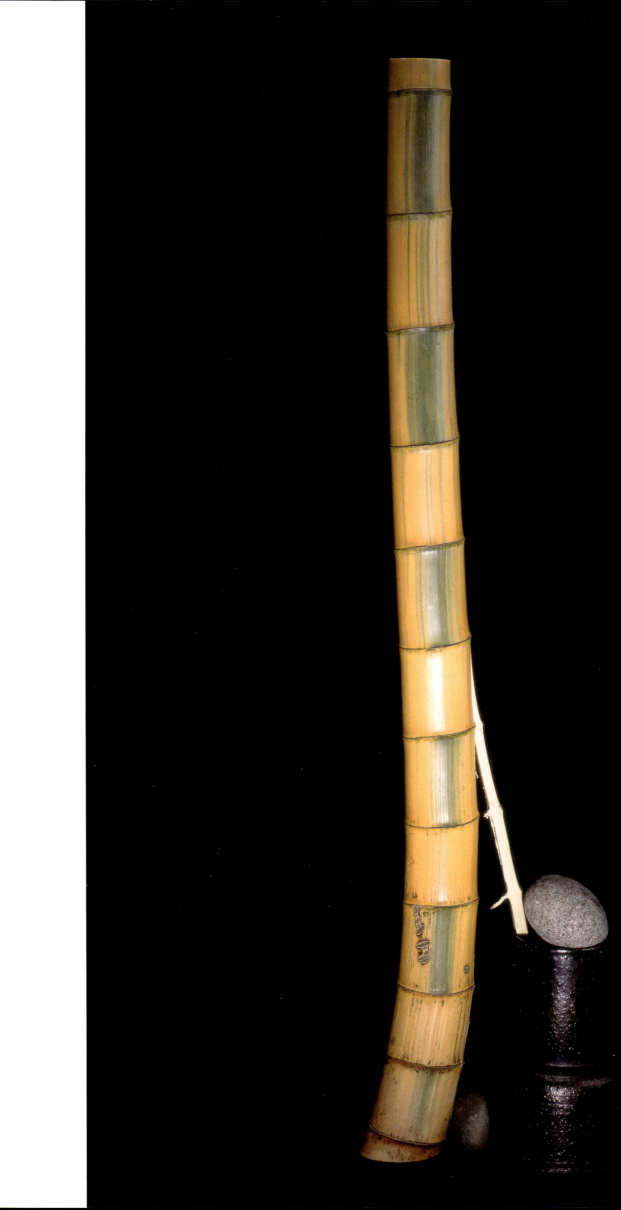

Familiar Forms

Many of my works are familiar objects such as sofas, beds, dresses, etc. These objects are a means of expressing my feelings, a tangible expression of my thoughts, a way of making myself understood. The choice for one specific shape depends on my mental state, but I chose not to reveal my exact feelings at an exhibition. For me it suffices when people like my works and find them beautiful or interesting. Of course I'm happy when people understand the works on a different, deeper level, but this is not a must. A lot of effort goes into these works and it sometimes takes me more than one year to finish them. As I already said in the introduction, I am most happy when I am surrounded by plants. When I'm working intensely, I go into a trance; I can't hear anymore, my views become monochromatic and my fingers move at an incredible speed. I exhaust myself to the point of fainting. It's a great feeling.

the impossible sofa – [p38-41]
Rosa (thorns and branches) | 1300 x 2000mm | 1996
Chiba City Floral Museum

This sofa covered in rose thorns was requested by a museum. They specifically asked for a long-lasting floral art piece. Considering how the sofa has been exhibited for 13 years, I think I can safely say that I have succeeded in this goal. The materials I used are dried rose-thorns and old rose trees. When I created the work I had just started my career as a freelance artist and I was barely making a living. That is why I chose a sofa. A sofa is meant for relaxing, but I myself never had the time to sit down or to take a rest.
In spite of the 'do not touch' sign, some people still couldn't resist and as a result some patches of thorns are a bit shiny.

sleepless Tokyo beauty – [p42-45]
folding screen: Rosa (powder of red petals), 3300 x 5400mm; **iron bed** designed by Ryusaku Matsuda: 1500 x 2000 x 1000mm; **pillow, sheet:** Rosa (thorns); **floor:** Rosa (red petals); **chair** designed by Ryusaku Matsuda: Rosa (thorns), height: 1500mm | 2000 solo exhibition, Art Forum Yanaka, Tokyo

Because of my depression, my general health has been deteriorating since 1998. Many of my creations are the results of sleepless nights. The collage 'Sleepless Tokyo Beauty' was made as a reference to the Disney animation film, in which a princess sleeps in a rose-covered castle. The work was conceived as a stage play, with myself or another insomniac as the main character. Tokyo is a very stimulating and eccentric city, bustling with activity day and night, a paradise for sleepless people. Since the gallery had windows on both sides, I asked the owners to keep the lights turned on during night-time, so people passing by could take a glance at the 'Sleepless Tokyo Beauty'. In fact the work was especially intended for this purpose and I did not really care for people visiting the gallery by day.
This was probably my most demanding composition ever. In a mortar I ground ten thousands dried red rose petals. Both the folding screen and the blanket were dusted in rose powder that seemed to radiate mysteriously at night. The sheet, the pillow and the reverse side of the blanket were covered in rose thorns, shaped and arranged as if someone had been sleeping on them, the imprint of the head and body clearly visible. I have no idea how many thorns were used, but it took me about one year to make the piece. The next year I collapsed and found out that I was suffering from severe depression.

seven virgins – [p46-47]
dress: Dianthus caryophyllus (petals); **floor:** Dianthus caryophyllus (dried petals), Rosa (petals); **paper figures** created by Ryusaku Matsuda, 1500 x 5000mm | 1994 solo exhibitions, Maki Tamura gallery, Tokyo

I started working on this series in 1994, but I had already created something similar for a group exhibition in 1989. In floral magazines we often see garments made of flowers, but it was not my intention to simply make a 'piece of clothing'; to me these dresses symbolized womanhood. They are made from the dried petals of 50.000 red carnations. I started by making a paper pulp model of a female figure without a head or arms, next I sewed the dress and I glued the petals onto it one by one. I chose to use carnations because these flowers gradually change colour and are thus excellent to demonstrate the passage of time. I never intended to exhibit this piece only once;

right from the start it was my idea to show it on several occasions so that the transformation of the dresses would become evident. With this creation, I also wanted to show the different stages in the transformation from a girl to a woman. The girls are innocent and the colour of the dresses is fresh and bright pink.

Three months later. The young girls want to become members of society; the carnations starts to change colour and become dark red.

Six months after their creation the carnations change colour again as the young ladies become members of society.

Three years later. The girls have fully matured, some of them seek pleasure and have become prostitutes.

Seven years later, the carnation dresses are worn out. I myself was exhausted too, as I was suffering from severe depression at the time. I remade the dress and made another two. I put the ladies on iron beds on an iron floor in a darkened room, as if they were in agony or pain. I put an egg shaped object covered in rose dust next to their beds. To me these objects represented the isolated souls of these women wishing to be revived. In fact these three ladies were representations of myself facing death and the work was the embodiment of my own tormented soul. After the exposition I kept the three dresses and I'm planning to expose them one last time under the theme 'funeral'.

A New York gallery asked for 'something gorgeous', so I created these huge dresses covered in rose powder. The exhibition lasted for three months and as I expected the dresses changed colour as time went by. At the end of the exposition the bright pink garments had turned almost beige, as if the women matured and got sexier. I wonder how many people will have noticed this transformation, since not many people visit the same exposition twice.

This work was requested for a HIV prevention campaign. After leafing through several fashion magazines I found the perfect lips to copy. I modelled this piece after the lips of a very popular runway model. I dusted them with very fine, bright red rose powder and moistened them to go mouldy. Unfortunately the end result was too shocking to be used for the campaign. Of course I know that HIV isn't transferred by kissing, but I think it was an effective way to get the message across to the public.

determination to become a member of society – [p48]

debutante – [p49]

window prostitutes – [p50-51]

depression ward – [p52-53]
Dianthus caryophyllus (petals), Rosa (powder of red petals); **bed**: 1400 x 1800 x 1000mm; **body**: 1800mm; **soul**: 400mm | 2001 solo exhibition, Maki gallery, Tokyo

as time goes by. three sisters, old but beautiful – [p54-55]
Rosa (powder of red rose petals); paper figures and dress created by Ryusaku Matsuda | 2200 x 5000mm | 2003 Perfection/Impermanence, Glyndor Gallery, Wave Hill, New York

kiss of death – [p56-57]
Rosa (powder of red rose petals, moulded) | 600mm | 2000

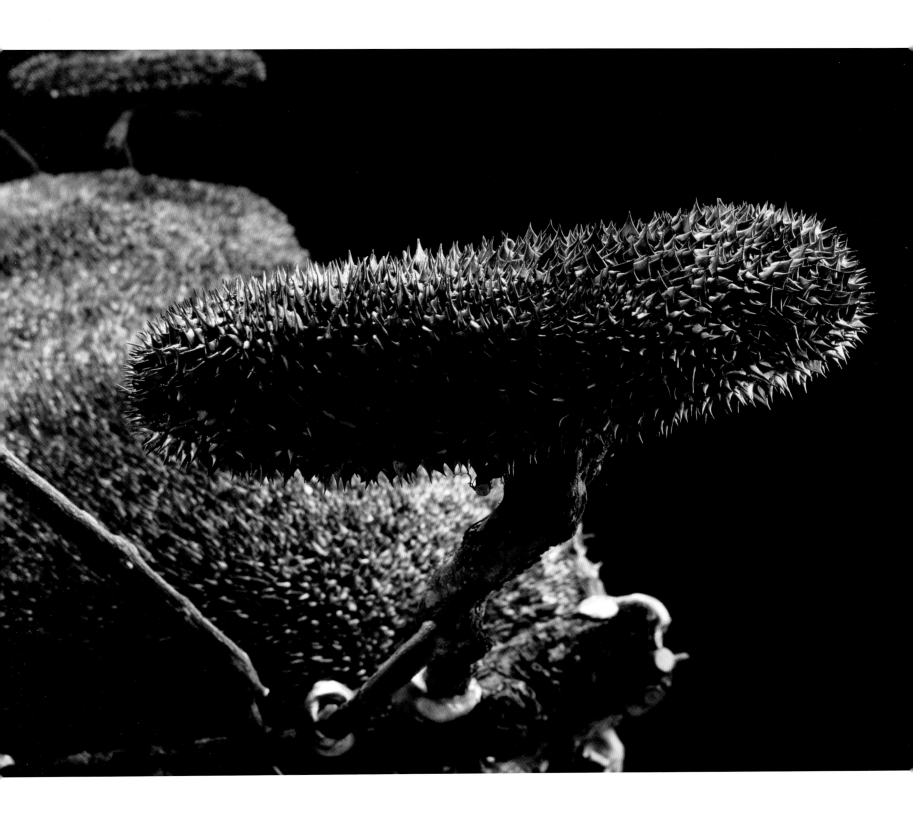

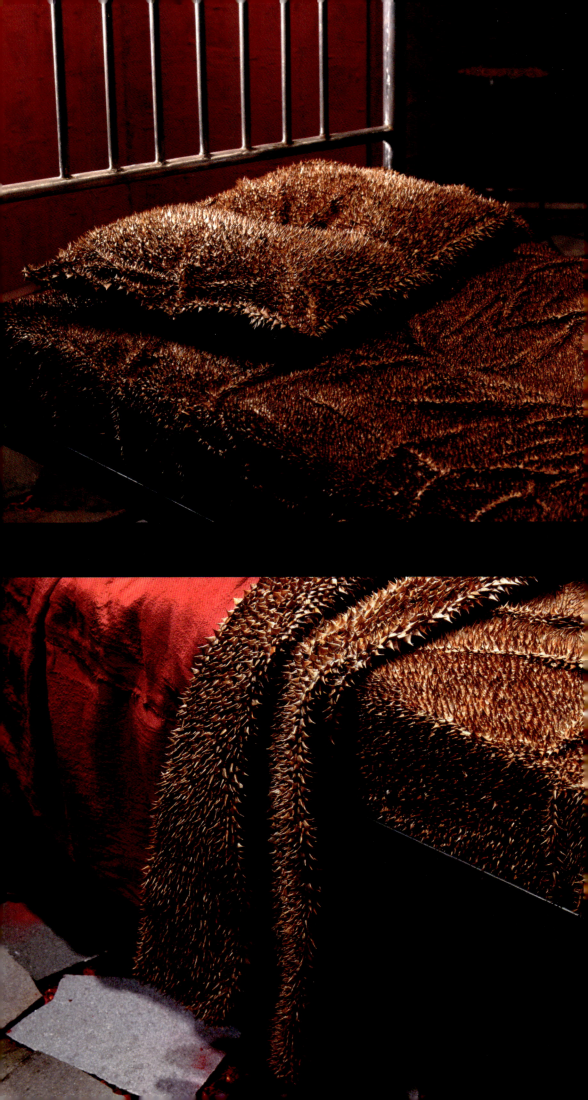

About Death

There is only one certainty in life: we will all die some day. I accepted this fate as a very young child, therefore I am not afraid of death. I was a sickly child, was hospitalized for a long time and faced death several times. I killed so many plants, just to express myself, that I believe I will have to make up for it, some-day, somehow.

the passing away of Buddha – [p59]
tower: Rosa (powder of red rose petals), 6000mm;
floor: Dianthus caryophyllus, Illicium verum, Limonium, Rosa, 10000mm | 2005 solo exhibition, Zenkoji Temple (world heritage site), Nagano

I am not a Buddhist, but neither do I deny this faith. Just like the people in Ancient Japan, my belief borders on Animism. Even though I am no Buddhist, I do have knowledge of this religion and with this piece I wanted to show my respect. Ikebana evolved from the flowers that were offered to Buddha and even before this, the Japanese held religious ceremonies in which flowers played an important role. This exhibition took place at a temple that is part of the UNESCO World Heritage, but does not belong to any religious denomination. Millions of people visit this temple every year. In this work I tried to interpret and express the moment of the passing away of Buddha. The shining tower covered in rose powder, is my image of Buddha's spirit ascending to heaven. On the floor around the tower, I scattered fresh flower petals according to the ancient myth that the gods used multi-coloured flower petals to celebrate the arrival of Buddha in heaven. I did not put any explanation next to the work, but saw people politely sitting around the piece and worshipping it. Instinctively they must have understood what I wanted to say. I was surprised that so many people appreciated my work. I felt extremely happy and embarrassed at the same time and kept bowing to them.

requiem for a rose – [p60-61]
tower: Rosa (powder of red rose petals), 10000mm;
floor: Dianthus caryophyllus (petals), Rosa (petals), 10m² | 1995 'Today's Japan', Sculptors' Center, Toronto

Going back ten years from the previous page, I was in good health. This exhibition took place in Toronto. I took the powder of ten thousand dried red roses with me on my journey to Canada, but collected the rest of the materials on the spot. The theme of the exhibition was 'Requiem'. Since I had 'killed' so many roses for my pieces, I decided to do a requiem for the beauty of my own art that had already required so many plant lives. I made two towers of ten meters high and dusted them in rose powder. Around these pillars, I put soil. The layer of soil was covered with dry petals of carnations and three thousand fresh rose petals. During the two months of the exhibition, the colour of the fresh petals faded, but to my great surprise and pleasure the soil underneath the pillars contained water and seeds and unexpectedly, sprouts started shooting up.

grave – [p62-65]
Rosa (powder of red rose petals, moulded)
1000 x 1500mm | 2001 solo exhibition,
Art Forum Yanaka, Tokyo

On this egg shape, I used bright rose powder, but I moistened it so it would go mouldy. I asked my friends to put a strand of hair and a piece of paper stating 'X will die one day' inside the egg. This practice is linked to gravestone wishing, but nor-mally one would wish for someone to come back to life. Of course I did not long for someone to die, I wrote my own name on the paper, but did not tell anyone.
Usually I do not put any explanation next to my works, because I do not want people to read, but to feel.

Why Watermelon?

That year, when I visited my mother at home, I collapsed. I could not eat or sleep and just wanted to die, but even lacked the willpower to do that. My mother took me to the hospital, but nothing was wrong with me physically. I was taken to a psychiatrist and was diagnosed with severe depression. The combination of medicine, rest and the loving care of my mother, made me want to go out again.

want to be free, but feel alone – [p67]
Citrullus lanatus (peeled), Musaceae (leaves)
300 x 600mm | 1999

we are free, I have got some friends in Tokyo – [p68-69]
Citrullus lanatus (peeled), Musaceae (leaves)
300 x 600mm | 2000

born as twins? – [p70]
Citrullus lanatus (peeled), jelly | 600mm | 2007

I remember – [p71]
Citrullus lanatus (peeled), jelly | 500mm | 2007

why was I alone? – [p72-73]
Citrullus lanatus (peeled), jelly | 600mm | 2007

One hot summer day I saw watermelons in my father's vegetable garden. The vines of the watermelons looked like chains and the melons looked like they were imprisoned. When I touched them, I could feel the scorching heat of the sun burning them and I just wanted to set them free and to free myself by doing so. Against the advise of the doctor, I returned to Tokyo and created this work. I wanted to give the melons wings to fly away. Since the scent of Musaceae leaves is the same as the one of watermelons, I used these as wings. I even peeled the melons to make their and my depression lighter. When I started taking medicine and got counselling from a psychiatrist, my depression cleared a bit but I still felt very lonely. Seeing the other depressed souls at the hospital, I realized I was not the only one who felt this way. The watermelons gave me the opportunity to start creating again. I could not take a rest or stop creating and I knew this was the way I should be living.

Peeling the watermelon was like going back in time, to the good old days of my childhood. I started thinking that if I kept on peeling, right to the red flesh, it might be possible to go back even further and maybe reach a time that does not exist in my memory. The time when I was still in my mother's womb. For a long time, I had been feeling that something was missing in my life, until one day my mother told me I was part of twins. While peeling the watermelon, I thought I could hear the heartbeat of my dead brother. When my mother passed away, I was sure my brother had been waiting for her to go up to heaven together. I really wanted to meet him, and I am sure both of them are waiting for me to join them in afterlife. I am certain that my life was already decided when I was born as the only surviving twin. I can not have the same ordinary feelings as other people or act like them. I only feel happy around plants. I feel that I live outside this world with the soul of my twin brother on my left shoulder.

Forms of Water

Water is essential to every living thing on earth. The human body and plants are similar, they both contain and need water. The growth and the shape of the body depend on the amount of water that is supplied. For me, every stage of the plant's life is interesting and beautiful, even when it has died and completely dried out. Especially the process of change and evolution excites me.

form of water I – [p75]
Musaceae (dried leaf, rolled), Scirpus tabernaemontani (dried) | 500mm | 2007

Looking at a banana leaf that was left over from one of my workshops, I found beauty in the changing colour of the dying leaf. It was striking. When it had gone completely soft, I decided to dissect it. Taking out the core and rolling it up, I found another kind of beauty. I rolled up many leaves and put them in a box. One week later they were a little mouldy, but I was impressed by their colour. Water had evaporated, the leaf had been nothing more than water in a special shape. This impression made me start working on the following pieces.

form of water II – [p76]
Musaceae (dried leaf and core) | 600 x 350mm | 2007

form of water III – [p77]
Musaceae (half dried leaf), Scirpus tabernaemontani (dry and fresh), Dahlia | 600 x 600mm | 2006

I started practising Ikeru with fresh, half dried and dry materials. I like all three stages of the plant, so I felt very privileged to work with these different materials. Fresh greens need water, but dried ones can be placed anywhere, so I put the dry materials up in the air. The half dried banana leaf was hung up just as it was, but the fresh Dahlia and Scirpus would undergo a process of change. Three different forms of water by plants.

form of water IV – [p78]
Phytolacca americana (juice) | 400mm | 2003

I picked berries of Phytolacca americana and kept them frozen. One day I defrosted the berries, made juice of them and poured it into a vase. Next, I put a piece of wood, wrapped up in Japanese paper, in the juice. After a short time, the juice started soaking into the paper, just like living plants soak up water.

form of water V – [p79]
grass | 150mm | 2002

After cleaning my garden, I looked into the dustbin and came up with a wonderful idea. I sorted out the grasses, added water and put them into the blender. After mixing, the liquefied grasses were put into plastic bags and frozen. This photo was taken one week later on the exact same spot as the grasses had been growing. The green ice cubes, shining like beautiful emeralds under the summer sun, melted quickly and disappeared into the soil. That way, I gave back to the earth what I took from her.

form of water VI – [p80-81]
Alocasia macrorrhiza (leaf and stem) | 500mm | 2007

This Alocasia macrorrhiza leaf was a left-over from one of my workshops. Looking at the cut end of the stem, I saw tiny drops of shiny liquid appear. I cut the stem in very thin slices and held them up to the light. It was so beautiful that I placed several slices on the leaf and asked a photographer to take a picture. One month later, the slices of stem had got very small and although its shape had not changed too much, the colour of the leaf was completely transformed. The dried pieces of stem shone like diamonds! I was very pleased by the changes time had brought along.

form of water VII – [p82-83]
Rosa (thorns) | 700mm | 2000

Although I was unpleasantly surprised by its price, I could not resist buying this beautiful vase from one of Japan's most famous ceramists. I enjoyed looking at it for several months before even starting to think about what type of plant to use it for. One day I poured water into it, and to my surprise and amusement, it could only contain very little water before overflowing. Still, I did not regret buying it and stuck to the original plan of arranging flowers in it someday. Being very sarcastic, I covered the part of the vase that could contain water, but the part, where water was spilling over, I adorned with rose thorns. Another shape of water, inspired by the vase.

The Spirit of Trees

Global warming is gradually changing the face of the earth. I already see the environmental changes in my home country. It looks like Japan has a very rich and diverse nature and is full of greenery but I have seen the mountainside transform before my eyes. The original vegetation of Japan is disappearing and instead cedars or Japanese cypresses, imported from other countries, are planted. Hence, the trees cause environmental disruption in two countries. Once planted, these 'imported forests' are left alone and are thus useless. A big mistake of Japanese forestry policy!

This piece was shown in the same temple as the work on page 59. By stripping the tree of its bark, I wanted to express the pure state of mind of the people visiting the place for worshipping. I wished to portray them as pilgrims. During the exposition, I had the strange feeling that something was wrong, but I could not quite put a finger on what it was. Later, when a gallery requested the pieces for another exhibition, I found out. While I thought the work was 'just' peeled tree, they used my works to incite the environmental debate. Although my work was esthetical and beautiful, I realized how selfish I had been, killing so many trees for my works. Something I cannot avoid as long as I am working with plants and other natural materials. I also came to the conclusion that until then, my art had mainly centred around me, while it is the task of the artist to demonstrate conscience about political and social topics too.

Angered and saddened by these new insights, I created this piece. As a protest against my chiselling of the tree, I made this collage from left-over bark and other pieces of tree that were wasted. After the exhibition I received several comments on the piece, some even thought it was scary and weird, but I think I did it right.

The work 'village conference at midnight' was exhibited at an international art festival held every three years in the scarcely populated mountain village of Niigata, where I was offered an old abandoned house to work in. Even in this faraway place, the original vegetation had almost disappeared and had been replaced by 'foreign' species. When I explored the woodland around the village, I still found twenty-two kinds of vernacular trees. From each one, I broke off a branch that I scraped and peeled. To me these represented the spirits of the trees. I installed them comfortably in a circle on Japanese cushions. It looked like they were gathering under the light of Japanese candles, just like the people of the village would have come together to talk. I wondered what they would talk about. We all live in different environments, circumstances and situations and each of us has to act accordingly. As I am one of the people working with plants, I felt that it was my duty to reflect on the feelings and thoughts of these trees.

protest demonstration of the spirits of the trees

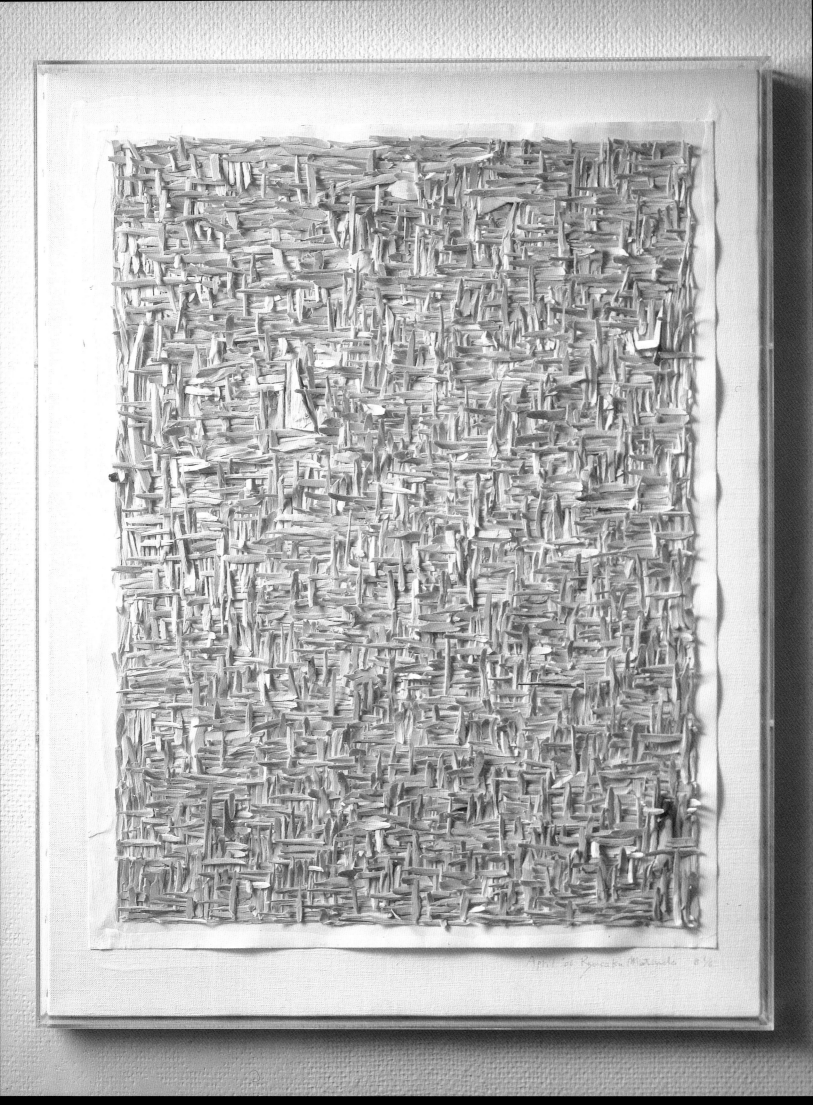

Cannot Live Alone

None of us live in a vacuum. Everyone is connected to something or someone and part of a bigger whole. This is the concept behind the creation of the works that follow. It's an idea I have been toying with for a long time.

sofa for lovers – [p95]
Enkianthus, strings | 1500mm | 1988 Ikebana Today,
Seibu department store, Tokyo

This chair is made of two hearts. The grey heart symbolizes young boys, the red heart stands for girls. Because they do not know love yet, both hearts are separated. But one day they will get together.

family sofa – [p96-97]
Enkianthus, strings | 1200 x 6000mm | 1988

This sofa can seat seven people at the same time: my four grandparents, my parents and I. I think this is the closest (minimum) blood relationship. I chose red and blue because these are the colours of the blood as represented on an anatomy doll. If I trace my past and all my current relations, I am connected to so many people, all together we could possibly connect to every human being on earth. This also means that everybody is distantly related or belongs to the same family. Why should we even fight or have wars? Unfortunately, I do not have children so my relationship will end, but my niece and nephew will continue the bloodline.

bamboo thoughts – [p98-99]
Phyllostachys (branches, powder of leaves), strings
40pieces, 3300mm | 1997 solo exhibition,
Art Forum Yanaka, Tokyo

For this work, I wanted to use every part of the bamboo plant; not only the stem, but also the leaves and roots. Unfortunately, the art gallery was too small to go ahead with the original plan. I cut all bamboos into pieces of three meters high and stringed them together. The roots were cut in five centimetre pieces. The leaves were dried and ground into powder that I scattered on the gallery floor. That way, I managed to fit all the bamboo into the small gallery. Achieving this felt like a symbolic gathering of the bamboo family.

we cannot live alone – [p100-102]
different types of branches, strings | 3300 x 2500mm
1996 solo exhibition, Art Forum Yanaka, Tokyo

It took me more than ten years to gather all material used in this piece. It was my idea to make this work from branches that no one else wanted and had no other specific purpose. Not one of them was bought. Some were left over from my workshops or artworks, other fell down in typhoons or were trimmed from roadside trees. When they heard about my plan, florists from all over the country sent me branches that would otherwise have been wasted. So this work was in fact created collectively, an endeavour of the minds of many people. With this work I want to show the universal bond between all living things. Now that we see our climate and environment change, we have to realize this once more. This is why I insisted to have this work included at the end of the book.

Epilogue

I still struggle with depression, but I keep fighting for life and for my artworks. I have never stopped creating. Some of my works may show the signs of my illness, but on the other hand, perhaps it was only possible to create them because of it. Whatever it is, I am sure that my depression matured me and let me grow. And that is what I will always strive for .

Acknowledgements

First of all I would like to express my gratitude to the readers of this book. You have just witnessed an artistic journey of more than thirty years. I would like to know what you think of it.

I want to thank the following people:
My parents, my father of ninety years old (and still living independently) and my mother, who passed away five years ago. From them, I inherited my love of plants, for which I cannot be grateful enough.
My teacher, Mrs. Mami Kawasaki, who taught me how to connect with plants with all my heart.
My interpreter, Mr. Tomoki Jchiyama, who translated my difficult Japanese into English so I could make my heart known to people all over the world
My publisher, Mr. Karel Puype, who understood me well and made great efforts to publish this book.
My photographers, for giving me the opportunity to show these works that will disappear one day. I could only make this book because of you.

Works and Words:
Ryusaku Matsuda
STUDIO MATSUDA 93
106, 6-27 Shinogawa-Machi
Shinjuku-ku Tokyo 162-0814 JAPAN
Phone & Fax 81-3-3266-1986
Mobile Phone 090-3292-1711
e-mail ryuusaku_m93@hotmail.com
http://matsuda93.hp.infoseek.co.jp

Photography
Kiyokazu Nakajima
p9-17, 24-26, 28-31, 35, 38-45, 52-53, 56-57,
59, 62-65, 67-83, 85-88, 90-93, 95-102
Kenichi Ogoshi
p18-23, 27, 32-34, 46-51, 89
Becket Logan
p54-55
Yoichiro Hinata
p60-61

Final Editing
Katrien Van Moerbeke

Layout and Print
Group Van Damme, Oostkamp (BE)

Published by
Stichting Kunstboek bvba
Legeweg 165
B-8020 Oostkamp
Belgium
Tel. +32 50 46 19 10
Fax +32 50 46 19 18
info@stichtingkunstboek.com
www.stichtingkunstboek.com

ISBN 978-90-5856-299-9
D/2008/6407/37
NUR 421